A Gift of Love

To: _____

From: _____

Date: _____

Mothering

Becoming the Heart of the Home

Written and Compiled by

Rosalie McPhee

Cover painting by Michael O'Brien

Design by Rob Huston

First Printing, September 8th, 2000
Feast of the Birth of Mary, Mother of God

Printed in Canada

MADONNA HOUSE PUBLICATIONS
COMBERMERE • ONTARIO • CANADA • K0J 1L0

www.madonnahouse.org

To all mothers,

*That they may know
the hidden glory of their vocation*

The Little Mandate

Arise—go! Sell all you possess. Give it directly, personally to the poor.

Take up My cross (their cross) and follow Me... going to the poor... being poor... being one with them... one with me.

Little, be always little! Be simple... poor... childlike.

Preach the gospel *with your life*, without compromise! Listen to the Spirit, He will lead you.

Do little things exceedingly well for love of Me.

Love... love... love... never counting the cost.

Go into the marketplace and stay with Me. Pray... fast... pray always... fast.

Be hidden. Be a light to your neighbor's feet. Go without fears into the depth of men's hearts. I shall be with you.

Pray always. I will be your rest.

The Little Mandate was given to Catherine Doherty from the Holy Spirit as she listened intently to hear how God wanted her to live the Gospel. Many others have heard the echo of these words in their own hearts and also endeavor to live them.

Table of Contents

Introduction

One of the most significant discoveries in my life was that motherhood itself is a way to holiness, and that it is the way of Nazareth. Christ's hidden thirty years in his hometown sanctified ordinary life for us all. Although he was God, and had the colossal task of redeeming all of stubborn humanity, he spent thirty years in a hidden carpenter's shop, learning a trade from his foster father.

I was a mother of young children when I first encountered Catherine Doherty's spirituality, and saw it lived at Madonna House. Something resonated deep within me, in that place where doubts and insecurity plagued my identity as a mother. Although I loved my family, I needed to hear that this was a worthy, holy vocation, and that I had been called to it by God himself. It was comforting to learn that He had extraordinary graces to give me, to see me through whatever I might encounter in that vocation.

Do little things exceedingly well for love of God...

The duty of the moment is what you should be doing at any given time, in whatever place God has put you.

These words sang in my heart, and gave me a new eagerness and excitement in responding to God's call. Following the example of His mother, I began to fulfill my humble daily tasks with new joy.

I read Catherine's books hungrily, and was able to apply so much of what I read to my own life as a mother. It made me more aware that everything we do can be offered to Christ, and can be a prayer. It was quite a revelation to me that the more monotonous the task, the more opportunity for prayer, because the mind is free to fix on God.

Catherine Doherty knew what it was to be a mother, not only to her own son, but to her many spiritual children. She was able to illuminate the ordinary, inspiring us to find God in the day-to-day joys and difficulties of family life.

Today families are looking for a spirituality that challenges them, meets their deepest yearnings, and addresses the struggles inherent in modern family life. Catherine's Little Mandate offers a faithful but radical spirituality for families, for living the Gospel is radical in today's world.

Our Holy Father, Pope John Paul II, has shown an extraordinary understanding and compassion for women, and a deep respect for motherhood. He tells us "the true advancement of women requires that clear recognition be given to the value of their maternal and family role, by comparison with all other public roles and all other professions." (*The Role of the Christian Family in the Modern World*)

Christ came into the world through the family, through the "yes" of a woman, when Mary became the mother of God and the mother of all. Never have we more needed such an attitude of faith in what we cannot see, as that which Mary showed in her unconditional response to God's will.

Today we have lost our appreciation and respect for motherhood, a vocation requiring so much tenderness, so much wisdom, and so many varied skills. We learn these in the school of love, and grow in holiness through our daily surrender to the will of our Creator, who continually fashions and molds us more and more clearly into His image. When God places us in a family, each of us is "hand-picked" for the others, to grow together in faith and love into an icon of the Trinity.

This book is designed for meditation and prayer. It is intended to offer inspiration and encouragement in the living of the vocation to family. *Mothering* is for those mothers who are looking for support and affirmation in their vocation, and who desire to embrace it more fully and completely, and "in this glorious and very hard vocation, to become saints themselves." (Catherine Doherty, *Dear Parents*)

By keeping our eyes on Mary and our hand in hers, echoing her *fiat* (yes) every day, motherhood will be restored, moment by moment, mother by mother.

Rosalie McPhee

Become God's Smile
upon the Newborn Child

God created man in his own image, in the image of God he created him; male and female he created them. And God blessed them, and God said to them, Be fruitful and multiply, and fill the earth and subdue it.

Genesis 1:27-28

I was expecting my fourth child when I came into the Catholic Church. I was hungry to learn and absorb all the riches of the Faith at once. As we entered Advent, and the expectancy of the coming of Our Saviour, I began to experience my walk with Mary.

Our baby was due shortly after Christmas, so as he grew inside me, I thought of her, holding in her womb the Saviour of the World. When I first felt my child move inside me, I imagined how it must have been to feel the first movements of her child who was God.

As my pregnancy advanced, and I began to experience more discomfort, I thought of her, riding eighty miles on a donkey to Bethlehem from Nazareth. I had nothing to complain about!

When our son was born two weeks early—on Christmas Eve—he crowned our Advent with his Christmas "presence". We named him Christopher after the One who gave him life, our mother Mary's Son.

Thank you, women who are mothers! You have sheltered human beings within yourselves in a unique experience of joy and travail. This experience makes you become God's own smile upon the newborn child, the one who guides your child's first steps, who helps it to grow, and who is the anchor as the child makes its way along the journey of life.

Pope John Paul II, Letter to Women

Pregnancy, an advent eternally renewed in every woman expecting a child, is a book written by the hand of God, with each page, each day, each hour, reminding us of the first Advent. Think of the first Advent now, when worlds were hushed and angels still . . . waiting, waiting for the answer of a young girl! Her *fiat*, spoken so softly as to be almost a whisper, shook heaven and earth, and began the ineffable, incomprehensible, most beautiful mystery of the Incarnation! Each pregnancy sings of the first Advent. Each is a time of waiting, of joy so immense that it can only be encompassed by the eyes and soul of a woman in love and filled with the fruit of that love.

Catherine Doherty, Dear Parents

It is a great honor to you who are married that God, in His design to multiply souls who may bless and praise Him for all eternity, causes you to co-operate with Him in so noble a work.

St. Francis de Sales

O Lord, I am filled with wonder at the wonder of you! You love me enough to share your own creative powers with me and my beloved, in co-creating new souls to live with you for eternity!

Make me a worthy vessel, my Lord. As I open my womb to "shelter human beings," may I also open my heart to them and to you.

Mary, my mother, show me how to "become God's own smile upon the newborn child," and to be "the anchor as the child makes its way along the journey of life." May I daily echo your fiat with my own, as I surrender my will to my Father's more completely every day.

Love... love... love... never counting the cost.

The Little Mandate

Mission of Service
and Love

Mary said, "Behold, I am the handmaid of the Lord. May it be done to me according to your word."

Luke 1:38

*W*e were at a wedding reception, sitting at a table with three other couples we had never met. My husband chatted easily with the person next to him, but I felt uneasy and out-of-place. I couldn't think of anything to say, and became irritated at how well my husband was blending in, laughing and at ease with everyone. Finally, the woman next to me, a beautiful, self-assured young woman, tried to draw me into conversation: "And what do you do?" she asked.

For a moment I couldn't think of a thing to say. What do I do? Have you got an hour, lady?! All the things I do in the course of a day... but would any of them seem important to her? How could I put into words the joy and fulfillment I experienced in mothering my seven children at home, and being home-school teacher to three?

I plunged in, as I began to speak openly of my life, my family, my motherhood, and all the little things I do. When I stopped speaking, there was a pregnant pause, and then she said pensively and sincerely, with tears in her eyes,

"How blessed you are..."

Mary's example enlightens and encourages the experience of so many women who carry out their daily tasks exclusively in the home. It is a question of a humble, hidden, repetitive effort, and is often not sufficiently appreciated. Nonetheless, the long years Mary spent in the house of Nazareth reveal the enormous potential of genuine love and thus of salvation. In fact, the simplicity of the lives of so many housewives, seen as a mission of service and love, is of extraordinary value in the Lord's eyes.

Pope John Paul II, General Audience, Jan. 29, 1997

Love is a fire. It must spend itself in service. Service is the dry wood for the fire of love that makes it burst into a bonfire that reaches into eternity and burns there...The very word "love" implies sacrifice and surrender.

Let us ask the Lord to show women the full-ness of the life at Nazareth. Pray that he might lift the veil of years and of sentimental piety, and present his own Mother as she really was--a housewife, a mother, a spouse, a woman busy at the sublime creative work of her kingdom, his home on earth.

Catherine Doherty, People of the Towel and Water

Christian wife! Follow in the footsteps of the ideal of all womanhood, the Blessed Mother of God; in joy and sorrow, she will be your advocate at the throne of her Son.

St. John Vianney

My Father in Heaven, you created Mary to be the mother of your Son, and to show all mothers how to live this holy role to the fullest. Give me the grace for the "hidden, repetitive effort" you ask of me as a mother and housewife.

Mary, may I embrace this "mission of service and love" as you did, and approach it with peace and joy in my heart. May I empty myself of "me" and become God's vessel in serving my family in great love.

Be hidden. Be a light to your neighbor's feet.

The Little Mandate

The Duty
of the Moment

Whatever you do, do from the heart, as for the Lord and not for others.

Colossians 3:23

I had my day planned out, and was energized to accomplish my long list of things. I had been putting off tackling the fridge—which had strange things growing in the back, threatening to take over. Once this was done, I could then go on to grocery shopping and restocking the fridge. There were bills to pay, which couldn't wait much longer. The list went on and on.

Just when I had removed the entire contents of the fridge onto the kitchen table, I heard a plaintive little cry from the bedroom. My little four year-old was awakening, and I went in to get her up. When I entered the room, she was sitting up, with her arms outstretched, her face flushed and her eyes watering.

"Hold me, Mommy!" her little voice pleaded.

"Okay, just for a minute; Mommy has lots to do today. Let's get you dressed, and ready. You can play quietly while I do my work."

As I started to take her nightgown off, I noticed she was very warm, and listless.

"Just hold me, Mommy, please!"

My day was spent holding her, rocking her, reading to her: this was God's plan for my day.

Woman can only find herself in giving love to others.

Pope John Paul II, Dignity and Vocation of Women

Motherhood is woman's vocation. It is an eternal vocation, and it is also a contemporary vocation... We must do everything in order that woman may merit love and veneration. We must do everything in order that children, the family and society may see in her that dignity that Christ saw.

Pope John Paul II, General Audience, Jan. 10, 1979

The duty of the moment is what you should be doing at any given time, in whatever place God has put you...

If you have a child, your duty of the moment may be to change a dirty diaper. So you do it. But you don't just change that diaper, you change it to the best of your ability, with great love for both God and that child. You can see Christ in that child.

Catherine Doherty, Dear Parents

Every moment comes to us pregnant with a command from God, only to pass on and plunge into eternity, there to remain forever what we have made it.

St. Francis de Sales

Lord, You have created me to love, and you chose each of my children just for me, to be loved by me and to be raised by me. May I embrace this holy and "eternal vocation" and believe in its dignity. Even when I feel unappreciated, may I always recognize in myself "that dignity that Christ saw." I offer all I do to you, for the salvation of my family.

Mary, my mother, be with me in all the little things I do throughout the day. Help me to know "the duty of the moment" in each moment, and to embrace it joyfully.

Do little things exceedingly well for love of Me.

The Little Mandate

Blessed are The Poor in Spirit, for Theirs is the Kingdom of Heaven

Therefore I tell you, do not be anxious about your life, what you shall eat, nor about your body, what you shall put on. For life is more than food, and the body more than clothing. Consider the ravens: they neither sow nor reap, they have neither storehouse nor barn, and yet God feeds them. Of how much more value you are than the birds!

Luke 12:22-24

What seemed like a tragedy was in reality an extraordinary and powerful blessing in the life of our family. Our house had burned to the ground that very day, and with it everything we owned. With no insurance, we were totally dependent on the grace of God and the generosity and love of a faith-filled rural parish. That evening, after driving over to look at the still smoldering remains of our home, we lay in bed in the farmhouse of a loving family who had taken us in. I could hear my children's soft, even breathing as they slept nearby, and there was a strange sense of peace and love.

Don and I spoke softly together, so as not to wake the children. "Shouldn't we be feeling devastated, afraid, distraught, or something—why do we feel this peace?" he whispered.

I looked at my newly baptized son who lay beside me. We had been alerted to the fire during the closing song of his baptismal service, as we held the baptismal candle and sang, The Light of Christ has Come into the World. *Though we owned nothing, we had everything we needed.*

Children must grow up with a correct attitude of freedom with regard to material goods, by adopting a simple and austere lifestyle and being fully convinced that man is more precious for what he is than for what he has.

Pope John Paul II,
The Role of the Christian Family in the Modern World

Poverty of Spirit—what does that really mean, in terms of a modern Catholic family? It means, first of all, utter detachment from all created goods. It means a deep, lasting realization that all created things, which include father, mother, children, relatives and friends—as well as money, house and goods—are given to us by God as means to one end, which is sanctity.

Catherine Doherty, Dear Parents, p. 87

Nothing created has ever been able to fill the heart. God alone can fill it infinitely.

St. Thomas Aquinas

Thank you for caring for us so lovingly, Lord. I'm sorry I take it for granted so often, and forget to thank you. I want to be a little bird in your hand. Rid me of the desire to have more; set me free from the lure of consumerism; forgive me for coveting what you have provided for my neighbors. Everything we have has been provided by you, and so is really yours, my Lord. Give me a grateful, humble heart, and lead me to be a good steward of all you provide us with.

Mary, my mother, help me to be poor in Spirit. Show me what it means for our family to turn to a more "austere way of life," and to find freedom in "utter detachment from all created goods." May I come to know the power and the peace of true sacrifice, and offer all to my Father.

Arise—go! Sell all you possess.
Give it directly, personally to the poor.

The Little Mandate

Tending the Sanctuary of Love

Like the sun rising over the mountains of the
Lord, such is the beauty of a good wife in a well-
run house.

Ecclesiasticus 26:16

*T*he knock on the door startled me. It was 10 am, and the house was an embarrassing mess. How could I get rid of this person? I opened the door a crack, hoping they wouldn't see what lay behind me. I saw the friendly face of my neighbor, and it hit me, like a bolt of lightning—This is Christ at my door! I'm shutting him out, just as the innkeepers did in Bethlehem! I opened the door wide, gave a smile of welcome, and invited her to sit down at the messy table. I put the kettle on for tea, and set about clearing the table and sweeping the floor, as I chatted with her. When I had finished that much, I sat down to have a cup of tea with her and to give her my full attention. She started to pour out her heart to me, and cry, and I listened and wiped her tears.

As she got up to leave, she said:

"I needed to share this with someone. I thought of you, just as I was passing your house. Thank you for listening. I feel so much better, and I think I can go home and start again. Thank you for welcoming me so warmly!"

If you only knew, I thought…

Motherhood must be treated in work policy and economy as a great end and a great task in itself. For with it is connected the mother's work in giving birth, feeding and rearing, and no one can take her place. Nothing can take the place of the heart of a mother always present and always waiting in the home. True respect for work brings with it due esteem for motherhood. It cannot be otherwise. The moral health of the whole of society depends on that.

Pope John Paul II, Homily, June 7, 1979

A home is not a dwelling built by hands. Rather, it is built by love, by that unity, that oneness, that will make out of a hovel a palace of joy and peace, because the tranquillity of God's order reigns in the heart of it.

Catherine Doherty, Dear Parents

Happiness is to be found only in the home where God is loved and honored, where each one loves, and helps, and cares for the others.

Blessed Théophane Vénard

Lord, you have given us this dwelling, and given me the task of making it into a home for our family. I invite you to live with us, and I pray for wisdom, guidance and strength to make it fit for you. Form me into the heart of this home, and make it a place where love dwells, a refuge from the storms of life. May I always see my motherhood as my primary vocation, and place all other aspects of my life in submission to this holy mission.

Mary, my mother, you made a home at Nazareth for your Son. Help me to make my home a sanctuary for my family, and to make it a dwelling for your Holy Family.

Go without fears into the depths of men's hearts.
I shall be with you.

The Little Mandate

Nourishing the Family
Transforming the Fruits of the Earth

Why spend money on what cannot nourish and your wages on what fails to satisfy? Listen carefully to me, and you will have good things to eat.

Isaiah 55:2

Give us each day our daily bread.

Luke 11:3

I'm trying to make dinner, if you would all just leave me alone!"

It had been one of those hard days, and I was feeling like I was going to explode. I was trying to get something on the table to feed my family, resentful that everything always fell to me, and all at once. The kids were fighting all around me, and I just couldn't deal with it. I stirred the cheese sauce with a vengeance, and noticed it was burned on the bottom. The vegetables were boiling over. Oh, if I could just get this meal over with!

I heard a little voice pierce through my black cloud of anger: "Hep oo, Mom?" My little toddler was looking up at me, reaching out to me in an embrace. I held him close, and felt a sudden calm.

As he set the table, his little tongue extended slightly, I watched him carefully put each thing in place. Some were backwards, but he stood back and looked with satisfaction at his effort.

"Jussa minute, Mom. Forget somepin."

He returned a minute later with a dandelion, and placed it carefully in a jam jar in the center of the table.

When you meet for meals and are together in harmony, Christ is close to you.

Pope John Paul II, Letter to Families

The Christian family will strive to celebrate at home, and in a way suited to the members, the times and feasts of the liturgical year.

Pope John Paul II,
The Role of the Christian Family in the Modern World

Of all things forgotten by us, the truly lost generation, is the breaking and eating of bread as a symbol of rest and re-creation. Eating is gathering together all the parts of ourselves that have been scattered throughout the day. We gather to be refreshed by the taking of food.

Every meal is a sacramental. It should be prepared with love and eaten in peace, because its purpose is to strengthen us for the service of Love—God.

Catherine Doherty, Dearly Beloved Vol. I

Whether a kitchen is very modern or very humble, people there lovingly and joyfully transform, transubstantiate the raw products of God's earth into food to feed their brothers and sisters. This is a service and a privilege almost beyond compare.

Catherine Doherty, People of the Towel and Water

What a tremendous responsibility it is to feed my family, Lord. It's not the time and effort it requires as much as the realization that their health depends so much on what they put into their bodies. There is so much to know and to learn: show me where to look and teach me what I need to know. Help me to see that "every meal is a sacramental," and to learn how to "transubstantiate the raw products" of your earth into food to feed my family.

Mary, my mother, show me how I can help our meal times to become times of sharing, where love and harmony can reign. May I prepare meals with love and care, so that my family may feed on my love.

Go into the marketplace and stay with Me.
Pray... fast... pray always... fast.

The Little Mandate

Teacher in the
School of Love

Train up a child in the way he should go, and when
he is old he will not depart from it.

Proverbs 22:6

I weeded the garden furiously, my mind weighed down by a feeling of inadequacy as a mother. My husband and I felt it important to teach our children the faith at home, especially in preparation for the sacraments. After all, we were the "primary educators" of our children.

It was a few weeks from my daughter's First Communion, and I realized how far behind we were in our preparation. Was she anywhere near ready? How could I be so irresponsible?

Somehow, we got through the lessons, and I relished the special time spent together. However, doubts still assailed me the night before. Had we done all we could? Was she ready?

At daybreak, I awoke to the realization that this was it; there was no more time. I went into her room to wake her. She was sitting, fully dressed, peacefully looking out the window. She looked up at me, her eyes sparkling with anticipation, and said to me:

"Mommy, I just can't wait to receive my Jesus!"

In the family women have the opportunity and the responsibility to transmit the faith in the early training of their children. They are particularly responsible for the joyful task of leading them to discover the supernatural world. The deep communion uniting her with them allows her to guide them effectively to Christ.

Pope John Paul II, Gen. Audience, July 13, 1994

Slowly, we begin to understand that the Catholic faith is not only a matter of attending Mass on Sundays and doing the bare minimum our Church requires, for even these practices of Catholicism are but means to an end. Living the Catholic faith is a way of life that embraces every minute of our waking and sleeping hours and permeates our lives at work, at home, in school, on a date, from the cradle to the grave.

Catherine Doherty, Dear Parents

I myself had then the gift of faith, so had every one in the house except my father, but he never was able to weaken the influence of my mother, which was so overpowering from the force of her example, that he could not succeed in turning me away from a firm belief in the Saviour whom he ignored.

St. Augustine, Confessions

Lord, you are the teacher. I need you to show me how to teach my children, especially how to lead them to "discover the supernatural world." May I discover the "deep communion uniting" me with them, and may it be deepened and strengthened as I strive to "guide them effectively" to you. Teach me all I need to know.

Mary, my mother, how must it have felt for you to teach God himself his own truths! May this become a "joyful task" for me, and for them, as I enter more deeply into this school of love.

Preach the gospel *with your life,* without compromise! Listen to the Spirit, He will lead you.

The Little Mandate

The Cross of Love

I have been crucified with Christ; it is no longer I
who live, but Christ who lives in me.

Galatians 2:19-20

Then Jesus told his disciples, "If any man would
come after me, let him deny himself and take up
his cross and follow me. For whoever would
save his life will lose it, and whoever loses his life
for my sake will find it."

Matthew 16:24-25

*M*y heart sank as I saw the body brace that had been custom-made for my 12 year-old daughter. It looked like an item of mediaeval torture, hard plastic that stretched from below her hips up to her underarm. Tears which I had held back since she had first been diagnosed with scoliosis sprang into my eyes. I quickly brushed them away, as I glanced at her to see her reaction. She seemed to accept it better than I did, and waited patiently while the doctor showed it to us.

He explained how she had to wear it 22 hours a day, with two hours off to wash and air out her skin. She was to wear it with a cotton undershirt to absorb the sweat, and would develop open sores on her hips, which would eventually harden into calluses with proper care.

It wasn't until he made her go down on her hands and knees on the floor and put it on, placing his foot on her back to tighten the leather straps with all his strength, that her tears started to flow, at first quietly, but then in sobs as we held each other—mother, father, and daughter—and wept.

Jesus' mission is expressed in the language of love. Indeed, the Sacrifice of the Cross is wholly wrapped in love; and from love it draws its most profound meaning.

Pope John Paul II, Homily, Sept 14, 1986

Offer your work, problems, difficulties, joys and pains to the Lord. He has many uses for your offerings in order to restore the world of souls to Himself.

Catherine Doherty, People of the Towel and Water

The price of souls is high—*high as a cross on which we must hang.*

Catherine Doherty, Staff Letter

I tell you that you have less to suffer in following the Cross than in serving the world and its pleasures.

St. John Vianney

Bear the Cross and do not make the cross bear you.

St. Philip Neri

Lord, when I gaze at you on the Cross, I see love—a love I want to learn, a love I want to strive to live. You have chosen my own crosses, tailor-made for me; help me to embrace them with joy, not just with resignation. I offer everything to you for the salvation of my family.

Mary, my mother, how familiar you are with the Cross. Although you had been warned of the pain, how your heart must have cried out in the agony of watching your Son's suffering. Teach me to accept my own crosses gracefully, and to help my children to bear their own.

Take up My cross (their cross) and follow Me...
going to the poor... being poor...
being one with them... one with Me.

The Little Mandate

A Mother's Prayer
Intercession of Love

In everything, by prayer and petition, with thanksgiving, make your requests known to God. Then the peace of God which surpasses all understanding will guard your hearts and minds in Christ Jesus.

Philippians 4: 6-7

Sometimes I felt like my whole life was out-of-control from the moment I opened my eyes in the morning. With teenagers now, as well as babies and toddlers, there was no longer a hush that descended in the evenings. I was stumped to find a quiet time to pray.

One morning in the midst of all the chaos—looking for shoes, ironing a shirt, getting breakfast ready, feeding the baby—it suddenly hit me. My prayer time was waiting for me—but I'd been too busy avoiding it to see! The fearsome solution was to get up before my children! To set the dreaded alarm, and get up half an hour before their usual waking time. I didn't know if I could do it, but it seemed to be the obvious answer.

At first it took tremendous effort, but after a while, I started to go to bed a little earlier, and waking became easier. This special morning time of peace allowed me to pray for my family, and to set the stage for the day. Even though I now love and depend on this time in the morning to get me through the day, you know what? I'm still not a morning person...

Where two or three are gathered in my name, there am I in their midst.

The family as the nucleus of society is a living stone of the ecclesial community and at the same time the primary place of prayer. The Second Vatican Council says, "With their parents leading the way by example and family prayer, children and indeed everyone gathered around the family hearth will find a readier path to human maturity, salvation and holiness."

Pope John Paul II, Homily, Sept. 9, 1985

Prayer is sometimes the fantastic movement of a dancer. Sometimes it is stone-like—the stillness of a person utterly immobile, lost in regions that few men reach but which many desire. Prayer is sometimes the babbling brook of a child or like the words of old people. Prayer is the words of men, women and children who know God and so easily talk to him!

Catherine Doherty, The Gospel Without Compromise

During the course of the day, recollect as often as you can that you stand in the presence of God.

Consider what He does and what you are doing. You will find His eyes turned towards you and perpetually fixed on you with an incomparable love.

St. Francis de Sales

Lord, you created my family as a "living stone of the ecclesial community," and the "primary place of prayer." Help me to order my life in a way in which prayer holds precedence. Help me to "lead the way by example" through my fidelity to my own personal prayer.

Mary, my mother, help me to be faithful in interceding for my family, as you intercede for all your children. Help me to persevere until they reach Heaven, and to do that, please help me to get to Heaven.

Pray always. I will be your rest.

The Little Mandate

Discovering Joy

Rejoicing in the Lord must be your strength!

Nehemiah 8: 10

*M*ommy, come play with me!" My little daughter's voice pleaded with me, for the third time in ten minutes. I glanced over at the huge mound of dirty laundry, the dishes stacked by the sink, and the things scattered across the floor. She was tugging at my skirt insistently, and my irritation was growing.

Worn down by her persistence, I finally looked to see what it was she wanted me to play with. She had been carefully arranging her Little People in their house. I started to half-heartedly move the figures around, feeling foolish, and wanting to get this over with. She looked over at me. "Mommy, your not playing attention!"

I was down at her level, but I realized with chagrin that I didn't know how to play.

"Can you show me how, Becky? I want to learn from you."

I watched this intricate lived-out drama as she moved the Little People around, making them interact with one another in strangely familiar ways. After watching for a while, I was ready to join in—this time with new joy in my heart.

Count it all joy, my brethren, when you meet various trials, for you know that the testing of your faith produces a steadfastness. And let steadfastness have its full effect, that you may be perfect and complete, lacking in nothing.

James 1: 2-4

There is needed a patient effort to teach people, or teach them once more, how to savor in a simple way the many human joys that the Creator places in our path: the elating joy of existence and of life; the joy of chaste and sanctified love; the peaceful joy of nature and silence; the sometimes austere joy of work well done; the joy and satisfaction of duty performed; the transparent joy of purity, service and sharing; the demanding joy of sacrifice.

Pope Paul VI, On Christian Joy

Joy is very quiet. It is like a light that shines in the darkness. It is connected with hope and with love. It is full of wonderment... When the bed is still very warm and I am half awake, joy comes to me every morning with the incredible thought that here God has granted me another day to love him and to serve him.

Catherine Doherty, Dearly Beloved I

A cheerful and glad spirit attains to perfection much more readily than a melancholy spirit.

St. Philip Neri

Lord, teach me about joy. I know that joy isn't "keeping a stiff upper lip," or always having everything go my own way. I need to learn joy, to "savor in a simple way the many human joys" that you place in my path. Open my eyes to recognize you in everything that happens to me, and to learn to see the way you provide, to see me through the difficulties.

Mary, my mother, I think of you as radiating joy and serenity. It doesn't mean you were always laughing, although I believe you had a light and merry heart. Help me to learn childlike wonderment, and to notice the beauty all around me. Instead of seeing the glass half-empty, help me to see the glass half full.

Little—be always little! Simple... poor... childlike.

The Little Mandate

Prayer of a Mother and Her Child

My child, whose body dwelt within my own, I lift you up to the One who created you. As you nestled next to my heart, when my womb was your world, our souls touched and came to know one another.

I give myself to you, my little one. You will always be my little one, even when the years disguise this truth. I offer my life for you, just as I offered my body to be your dwelling and your sustenance. I will be your mother for eternity, and I will do all within my power to help you get to Heaven, as I know you will help me, whether or not you intend to.

Mary, mother of mine, be a mother to this child. Show me how to love more deeply, more purely, more completely, and so teach this little one the meaning of love.

Fruit of my womb, flesh of my flesh, let us continue on this journey of life and love. May the Holy Trinity draw us into that boundless pool of tenderness and mercy. May I truly "become God's smile" upon you, my precious, precious child.

Do <u>you</u> have a story?

You can help our apostolate in our mission to spread the Gospel by sharing your stories with us!

We invite you to send us your personal accounts of true incidents in your own family life that illustrate the living of "The Little Mandate."

Please send your story to:

> Madonna House Publications
> Attn: Little Mandate Books
> 2888 Dafoe Rd
> Combermere ON   K0J 1L0
> Canada

Please be sure to include your return address.

Notes

Notes

Acknowledgments

We would like to express our gratitude to the following publishers for permission to use quotations:

Tan Books and Publishers, Inc., Rockford, IL, for permission to quote from The Voice of the Saints © 1965 by Burns & Oates, London. Reprinted by TAN Books and Publishers, Inc., by arrangement with Burns & Oates Ltd.

Harmony Media, Inc., Gervais, OR, for permission to quote from The Teachings of Pope John Paul II on CD-ROM and The Illustrated Catholic Bible on CD-ROM.

Scripture quotations are taken from:

The New American Bible ©1991, 1986, 1970 by the Confraternity of Christian Doctrine, Washington, D.C., and are used by permission of the copyright owner. All Rights Reserved. No part of the New American Bible may be reproduced in any form without permission in writing from the copyright owner.

The Revised Standard Version of the Bible: Catholic Edition, copyrighted, © 1966, by the Division of Christian Education of the National Council of the Churches of Christ in the United States of America, and are used by permission. All rights reserved.

The New Jerusalem Bible, Reader's Edition, © 1985 by Darton, Longman & Todd Ltd. and Doubleday, a division of Bantam Doubleday Dell Publishing Group, Inc.

MADONNA HOUSE PUBLICATIONS

COMBERMERE • ONTARIO • CANADA • K0J 1L0

The aim of our publications is to share the Gospel of Jesus Christ with all people from all walks of life.

It is to awaken and deepen in our readers an experience of God's love in the most simple and ordinary facets of everyday life.

It is to make known to our readers how to live the tender, saving life of God in everything they do and for everyone they meet.

Madonna House Publications is a non-profit apostolate of Madonna House within the Catholic Church. Donations allow us to send books to people who cannot afford them but most need them all around the world.

Thank you for your participation in this apostolate!

How to Contact Us

Telephone:	1-613-756-3728
Fax:	1-613-756-0103
Address:	Madonna House Publications
	2888 Dafoe Rd
	Combermere ON K0J 1L0
E-mail:	madonnah@mv.igs.net
Web Site:	www.madonnahouse.org

If you enjoyed *Mothering*, we think you would also like:

Fathering

Building the New Civilization of Love

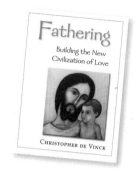

Fathers are invited to enter deeply into their father-hood in order to discover their true and most central vocation. This book offers concrete help and encouragement in living the gospel call to become transformed through loving their family.

In this book, you will find:

- Learning to love through a "very special form of personal friendship" with your wife.
- Being a "guardian of life."
- Allowing God to lead through you.
- Loving your family as Christ loved the Church.

Fathering features reflections and prayers written by Christopher de Vinck, the award-winning author of *The Power of the Powerless* and *Simple Wonders*. He is a regular feature writer for *Reader's Digest*, *Guideposts*, and *The New York Times*, and lives with his wife and three children in Pompton Plains, New Jersey.